Mackenzie Goode Makes a Mistake
A Big One
Judith Natelli McLaughlin

Mackenzie Goode Makes a Mistake, a Big One
Mackenzie Goode Series, Book 1
By Judith Natelli McLaughlin
© Copyright 2015 Judith Natelli McLaughlin

Published by Anaiah Adventures
An imprint of Anaiah Press, LLC.
7780 49th ST N. #129
Pinellas Park, FL 33781

This book is a work of fiction. All characters, places, names, events are either a product of the author's imagination or are used fictitiously. Any likeness to any events, locations, or persons, alive or otherwise, is entirely coincidental.

All rights reserved, including the right to reproduce this book or portions thereof in any form. For inquiries and information, address Anaiah Press, LLC. 7780 49th ST N. #129 Pinellas Park, Florida, 33781.

First Anaiah Adventures print edition September 2015
Edited by Anaiah Press, LLC
Book Design by Anaiah Press, LLC
Cover Design by Anaiah Press, LLC
Illustrations by Judith Natelli McLaughlin

For Maggie

ONE

Mackenzie Goode looked at herself in the bathroom mirror and tried to brush her hair for the first day of school. "Wrong," she said. "Just wrong." She used water. She used her sister's fancy hair gel. But *nothing* worked, and her hair wouldn't lie flat. Mackenzie was blessed with a great sense of humor, but had eight—count them, eight—cowlicks, those things that made her hair look crazy no matter how many times she brushed it.

On the first day of third grade Mackenzie's cowlicks were not agreeing with her at all, especially the one above her left ear. That's why she wore two pigtails every day in second grade. But this was third grade and Mackenzie Goode promised herself she *would not* wear pigtails in third grade. Pigtails were so last year. The kids would make fun of her. She would shoot a joke back at them. And who would get in trouble? Mackenzie. That's who. And *that* would be a mistake. And there was another thing Mackenzie promised herself: she would not make any mistakes in third grade. In second grade, she remembered making a lot of mistakes.

Mackenzie's Number One Second Grade Mistake? The time she shouted out without raising her hand to her teacher, Mrs. Reilly, "School is the opposite of fun!" Of course it was right after Mrs. Reilly said, "We have a fun assignment today, gang." Mackenzie didn't really mean it. She was just trying to make the other kids laugh. And it worked, too. They laughed. Every one of them.

I'm a funny kid, Mackenzie thought to herself with a smile. *I think I was born funny.* Mackenzie rummaged around her brain for a bit, but no matter how hard she tried, she couldn't come up with one memory of watching *Sesame Street*, *Arthur*, or even *Barney* on television. While other kids were busy with those "learning" shows, she was curled up on the couch with her dad watching the old-time comedy teams of

Laurel and Hardy or Abbott and Costello. She observed their jokes and their timing, but most of all, she and her dad just laughed. Mackenzie's Dad said she learned to make people laugh before she even learned the alphabet.

But back in second grade, Mrs. Reilly didn't think Mackenzie was funny. She timed her joke perfectly, too, but Mrs. Reilly didn't laugh. Instead, she put on her worst I-Told-You-So face and told Mackenzie that if she thought school was no fun that she, Mackenzie Goode, didn't have to do any work that day. In fact, she told Mackenzie to only do fun things. Sounds cool, right? Well that is what the worst I-Told-You-So-Face was for, because Mackenzie soon found out that what's really no fun is *not* doing work while every other kid *is*.

She asked Alison Greene to play Apples to Apples, but Alison said, "No, I have to finish this math sheet." She asked Kelly Byron to go to the reading corner and check out the funny knock-knock jokes she wrote last night, but Kelly said, "No, I have to finish my spelling." And she asked Randy Mooney if he wanted to feed Ruffles, Room Two's pet gerbil, but he said, "No, I'm finishing a science sheet."

That was the most no fun Mackenzie ever had. So she cried in front of Mrs. Reilly and the whole entire class. She didn't want to. In fact, she tried really hard to hold all those tears in, but the harder she tried the sweatier she got and the more those watery tears kept filling up in her eyes until finally she couldn't hold them back any more and they spilled all over her cheeks. That was two mistakes in one day! Wrong.

And when she got home from school that day the no fun continued. Mackenzie didn't want to, but she had to tell her mom about getting in trouble. Mom was *not* happy. Mom had to tell Dad and he was *not* happy either. Mackenzie was grounded forever—no play dates after school. Sure, her parents were sorry she cried in front of the entire second grade. And they even gave her great big Mom and Dad hugs, but she saw it in their eyes. Disappointment. Mac never wanted to be grounded again, but more than that, she never wanted to see that look in her parents' eyes again.

Mackenzie sighed big and loud. Then, she looked at herself, and her crazy blond hair, one more time in the mirror before promising herself out loud, "I swear on all my eight cowlicks that I, Mackenzie Goode, *will not* make any mistakes in third grade, because that would just be *wrong*."

TWO

"Mac, time for breakfast," Dad shouted from the kitchen. "I made your favorite."

Despite her crazy hair, Mackenzie smiled at herself one last time. This was, after all, the beginning of third grade! Head down, she raced out of the bathroom—silly for what she hoped were strawberry smoothies and blueberry pancakes—and crashed right into her older sister, Daphne. Mackenzie looked up. Daphne's outfit was Beautiful with a capital B! No surprise there. She was the total opposite of Mac. Great sense of fashion and fantastic hair: long, silky, and straight. But sorry to say, *no* sense of humor. "Wrong," Mackenzie whispered under her breath. But before Mackenzie had a chance to tell Daphne how pretty she looked or how sorry she was for crashing head on into her, Daphne screamed.

"Mackenzie Goode, you little twerp, you cannot go to school looking like—like—like—"

"Like what?"

"Like *that*!"

"*You* better learn to look where you're

going! Better yet, Daph, just go where you're looking." And with that, Mackenzie shoved Daphne into the bathroom, pulled the door shut and ran down the steps for breakfast, letting out loud, deep, and hearty laughs.

"Good morning, Daddy," Mackenzie said in her Sweet-as-Pie-and-Nothing-is-Wrong voice. She jumped into her seat at the table, which, she was happy to see, was set with a napkin and a strawberry smoothie.

"Mackenzie Goode, what happened up there?"

"Nothing important. Good smoothie."

"I'll tell you what happened," Daphne said, her face red with madness, just steps behind her sister. "I was just trying to help Little Miss Eight Cowlicks out when she totally shoved me into the bathroom. Look, I think she bruised my arm. If I can't try out for cheering today, it is *her* fault." Daphne glared at Mac with eyes as narrow as a folded envelope.

"Daph, are you exaggerating just a bit?" Dad said, giving his oldest daughter the first blueberry pancake and his youngest daughter a wink. "Mom!" Daphne screamed.

"I guess I'm not getting any more work done this morning," Mom said as she popped out from her office. "Daphne, honey, just relax. You're an eighth grader now. Don't let the little things bother you."

"Little? You call this mark little? Just look at what your daughter did to me!" Daphne said, shoving her arm into her mother's face.

"Oh, Daphne, please don't start. Not on the first day of school," Mom said. "Mac, exactly what is up with your hair? Can't we put it in pigtails? It looks so nice and neat that way."

"That's exactly what I said, Mother," Daphne said.

"That is *so* last year, Mom," Mac said, sticking her tongue out at Daphne. "I'm too old for that now."

"I tried to tell her, Mom," Daphne said. "But I got shoved into the bathroom. Be careful!"

"Pancakes, guys. Eat up fast. You have to do the Bus Stop Dash in five minutes!"

"Donald, did you have to make pancakes today? Seriously? I don't want to have to clean up this mess. I have a conference call and—"

"Clean up? What are you talking about? I always clean—"

"If cleaning means putting everything in the sink, you sure do. But I am left to wash the counters, rinse the plates—and oh, never mind." Mom tilted her head as she examined Mackenzie. "I have just the thing." Mom pulled out the junk drawer and fumbled around until she found what she was looking for.

"Daddy always cleans," Mac grinned big at her father.

"Perfect," Mom said, paying no attention to Mac, smiling at what she discovered in the junk drawer. She licked her fingers and marched over to Mackenzie. With a gob of saliva, she slicked back her daughter's hair and secured each side with a pink plastic barrette. "You look beautiful, nice and neat. Mrs. Kearny and all your friends will actually be able to see your pretty face."

"Much better, Mom," Daphne chimed in. "Little Miss Eight Cowlick wouldn't listen to me."

I look like a big fat baby, Mackenzie thought. *Wrong. A big fat baby with Mom's own brand of saliva hair gel. Yuck!*

"C'mon. Let's go, go, go! Time for the Bus Stop Dash. Get out there, you Goode girls, and have a great first day," Dad said, holding out paper bag lunches for Daphne and Mackenzie.

"Love you girls," Mom said.

With grace and ease Daphne slid out the door, a tiny smile on her lips. A grumpy Mackenzie followed behind. *First day of third grade and I look like a baby and smell like saliva. Wrong.*

THREE

"Mac! I saved your seat," Charise screamed out the window of the big yellow school bus. Charise Charbonneau—just seeing her smiling face made Mac happy. Everything about Charise made Mac happy, from reciting her poetic French name to sharing the silliest inside jokes, and there she was, waving her hands frantically, until she was sure her best friend saw her. Mac and Charise had been best friends since before they were born. They met when their mothers were pregnant and were born in the same hospital and on the same day!

"Cheese!" Mac said, feeling relieved as she skipped onto the bus. Cheese was the nickname Mac's dad gave Charise back when they were in pre-school. Mac and Cheese. They went perfectly together he said. He was right.

"Third grade, Cheese! How is it that we were swimming at the town pool yesterday and are back on the school bus today?" Mac said.

"I don't know," said Cheese. "What's wrong with you?"

"What do you mean?"

"You have that 'something's wrong' face on. I can tell," Cheese said.

"I do? Well, smell me," Mac said.

"Huh?"

"Smell my head. Do I smell like spit?"

Cheese held her breath and leaned in toward Mac's head.

"You can't smell me if you are holding your breath!"

"Oh, right. Sorry." Charise gave a quick sniff. "No, you smell fine."

"Good." Mac said, telling Charise about her mother's saliva hair treatment. "And the worst part is I already broke my promise."

"What promise?"

"I promised myself I would not make any mistakes in third grade and my hair is just one big, huge, smelly mistake!"

"Yeah, it is pretty, um—"

"Wrong?" said Mac.

"With a capital W!" Charise said.

"Can you believe Daphne thinks this looks good?" Mac said. "It's no wonder I had to shove her in the bathroom."

"You did what?" Charise said.

"Never mind. It wasn't even a shove. More like a gentle tap. But she deserved it."

Charise raised her eyebrows in disbelief.

"And then she got all wimpy on me crying about a bruised arm. But my hair! Charise, can you believe my crazy sister honestly thinks this looks good?"

"Actually, yes. I can believe it! Hey, where is she anyway?" Charise turned around, trying to spot Daphne. "Did she stay home to nurse that bruised arm?"

"Nah," Mac laughed. "Eighth graders go on a different bus. She's with the older kids now. Secret?"

"Of course. Capital S."

"You know I can't stand her, right?"

"Right."

"She's obnoxious and too pretty for her own good."

"Right."

"Well, I know this is going to sound crazy, but I kind of sort of miss her. I mean, I've never been on this bus without her."

"Know what? Me too."

"Really?"

"Really. But, look, Mac, we have each other. We'll be good!"

"Like Mackenzie and Daphne Goode," Mac said without missing a beat. To her delight, Charise laughed out loud but the laughter didn't last long.

"You know what Daphne told me?" Mackenzie, leaned in close to her friend, bringing her voice down to a whisper. "She said our teacher, Mrs. Kearny, is *really* hard. When Daphne had her, all the kids called her Captain Kearny, because she saluted them every morning."

"Really?"

"That's what Daphne said. She also said Mrs. Kearny doesn't wear real clothes. She wears a uniform. Like from the army or something."

"What?"

"I'm scared, Cheese."

"Me too. But at least we'll be together. I never thought they would put us together again after kindergarten. Remember when they caught us jumping off the sinks in the girls' room?"

"That was your idea, Cheese! But who got in trouble?"

"Oh, *mon cher*, it was you!" Charise said with a smile.

"*Mon cher*. That's 'my dear,' right? You're so lucky you speak French. It makes you sound so, so, so—cool! So not like me!"

"Listen, *mon amie*," Charise said, using her fancy French again. "I have just the thing to fix you up. It's a present and the timing couldn't be better," Charise said.

"Not another one," Mac said. "You already gave me my Parisian Bobblehead Doll. It looks great in my collection, by the way. Love the cap!"

"You mean *beret*! In French that is called a *beret*."

"*Beret*. Right."

"Look! I got this, too, while I was visiting my grand-mère Charbonneau in France this summer. All the kids in Paris are wearing them." Out of her Parisian pink, patent leather backpack Charise pulled a black silk headband with a big, huge bow. Smack in the middle of the bow was a big, huge, fake, capital D diamond.

"But Cheese, I can't. That's yours! Your grandma—"

"Grand-mère—"

"Yeah, grand-mère got that for you."

"Yeah, but I think you need it more than I do."

"What about Cowlick Number Eight? It's really being stubborn."

"Let me see." Charise said. She unclipped the barrettes, put them in her pocket and gently placed the headband on

Mac's head, making sure to capture at least three out of the eight cowlicks. "Perfect. Now you look like a third grader. No ponytails and no pink barrettes. Here, look," Charise said, holding up her backpack so Mac could see herself in the reflection of the patent leather.

She liked what she saw, nodding her head in approval. "How do you say perfect in French?"

"*Parfait.*"

"It's *parfait*! Mac smiled. "Third grade—ready or not, here we come."

FOUR

"Good morning, Kelly," Mrs. Kearny said. Mrs. Kearny was standing outside room 3K greeting all her students for the very first time. Mackenzie, who was closer to the back of the line than the front, noticed Mrs. Kearny was tall. Very tall. Mac thought if her third grade teacher were standing outside, her head would be in the clouds. And Daphne was right. She actually saluted each student!

Mac elbowed Cheese in the ribs when she saw it.

"Are we going into the third grade or the army?" Mackenzie whispered.

Cheese laughed, which made Mac happy.

Then Mac noticed it. Mrs. Kearny *was* wearing regular clothes. She wasn't wearing a uniform. Daphne was exaggerating. She got Mackenzie all worked up on purpose.

Mackenzie felt a bit of relief. She elbowed Cheese again. "Maybe Mrs. Kearny should trade in those clothes for a uniform. Compared to that outfit a uniform would look prettier."

Charise started to laugh but then Mac saw it. Charise's back got really straight and her body stiffened up. It was like

Charise was willing herself not to laugh at Mackenzie's jokes.

"Shh, Mac. This isn't the time for your jokes," Cheese whispered back. "It's the first day of school."

"Right. Right. Sorry, Captain Cheese," Mackenzie said, with a laugh and a little salute.

Charise giggled, then brought both hands to her mouth. Her eyes grew wide.

"Don't worry, Cap," Mac whispered in Charise's ear. "Mrs. Kearny is too busy with the front of the line to pay any attention to us in the back."

Charise let out a tiny sigh, but kept her hand over her mouth, just in case Mackenzie made another joke.

"Good morning, Alison," Mrs. Kearny said, loud enough for the whole line to hear. And there it was again, that little salute.

And then, Alison curtsied. She actually curtsied. Mackenzie thought she might throw up.

"Good morning, Mrs. Kearny," Alison said. "I am so happy to be in your class this year. My mom says you are the best third grade teacher. Can I be your helper today?"

"Well, I am so happy to have you in my class, dear. I'm not sure I need a helper today, but find your seat and I will keep you in mind for another day," Mrs. Kearny said.

And after Randy, Johnny, Tyler and Cheese, finally, it was Mackenzie's turn.

"Good morning, Mackenzie," Mrs. Kearny said. And there it was; that little salute.

"Good morning, Captain," Mackenzie said, a little giggle following, along with a little salute.

Mrs. Kearny just gave her a look. Not an awful look. Not a scary look. But one that said, "Try again." So she did.

"I mean Kearny," Mackenzie said, feeling just a bit flustered. "I mean Mrs. Kearny," she said finally, before running into the class, looking for Cheese.

Mac took a look around and really liked her third grade classroom. She liked the cursive letters on the wall, even though she was scared she would never, *never* be able to learn cursive. She liked how every subject had its own station set up in the four corners of the room. There was a math station with a huge poster above it: IT ALL ADDS UP!

There was a Science station with a sign: EXPERIMENT: The *I* in "experiment" was a test tube spilling over with lots of bubbly stuff. Mac really liked that. There was also a writing station: WITH WORDS ANYTHING IS POSSIBLE.

Finally, there was a reading station poster: TAKE A TRIP WITH A BOOK. Reading was Mac's favorite. She just knew she would spend a lot of time in the reading corner. She was happy to see beanbag chairs, bright red carpeting and a huge collection of books. She even noticed one titled *1001 Jokes and How to Tell Them*. She would have to borrow that one.

Mac found her desk in the back of the room, just the way she liked it. Her name was written in the most perfect cursive on a long sticker taped to her desk. And even better, Alison was in the front of the room and Cheese was right next to her, Mackenzie Goode. This was Awesome, she thought. With a capital A.

"Do you believe she put us next to each other?" Mac whispered to her best friend.

"I know. We won't even have to pass notes," Cheese whispered back. "We'll be able to talk just by looking at each other!"

"Okay, class," Mrs. Kearny said. "Glad to see all my students found their seats. As you probably noticed, your names have been written in cursive. That is because we are all going to learn how to write in cursive this year."

Alison's hand shot up in the air but she didn't even bother for Mrs. Kearny to call on her before she yelled out. "I already know how to write in cursive. My mom taught me over the summer. My mom says my penmanship," she took a break to stand and look around at the class, "that means my writing. My penmanship looks just like a grownup's."

Wrong! Mac thought, using her eyes to talk to Cheese.

Using her eyes, Cheese agreed.

"Very good, Alison. But, in my class, I would prefer if you waited to be called on before sharing, okay?"

Alison didn't even have the sense to turn bright red, Mac thought. She just said yes to Mrs. Kearny. Mac and Cheese stared at each other again, talking with their eyes.

"And another thing about my class, we will always be reading a book together. Always. At some point during the day we will join together on the red carpet and I will read out loud from an ongoing story. The first book up is called *Nothing is Impossible*.

Mac and Cheese used their eyes to shout out *yes*! This was going to be great! Maybe it was true. Maybe Mac could make it through third grade with no mistakes. After all, like the title of the book, *Nothing is Impossible*.

FIVE

"Okay, class, now that I told you about the math station, the science station, the reading station, and the writing station, why don't you all join me on the red carpet," Mrs. Kearny said. "Let's begin reading *Nothing is Impossible*. I am positive you will love this book."

"It's to the red carpet," Mac said. "Magic carpet rides for all!" Mac pumped her fist in the air, then pretended to fly to the carpet. "C'mon Cheese! Follow me."

"*Mais oui, mon amie!*" Cheese said, flying right behind Mac.

"Translation?" Mac asked.

"Ah, yes, my friend!"

"*Parfait*! Now bring it in for a landing, Charise."

"Can I read a page?" Alison asked. "My mom says I am a very good reader. I read on a sixth grade level."

Mac rolled her eyes at Cheese. Cheese rolled her eyes back. They were already seated, knee to knee, on the red carpet.

"She is just trying to show off," Randy said.

"Children, I do love your enthusiasm! But, if we are going to work together in 3K that means no calling out. Please remember to raise your hand and wait to be called on.

As for reading, there will be plenty of opportunities for you to read out loud in the third grade. But this is a chance for me to read to you. I want you to listen to the story and picture the characters in your very sharp brains."

The kids all sat criss-cross applesauce on the red carpet. Mac, next to Cheese, couldn't have been happier. Third grade. Best Friend. Good story. What could possibly go wrong?

Mrs. Kearny began to read. Mac got sucked right into the story. Just the first few paragraphs were all it took. But then, it happened. A loud, rolling, grumbling noise. Mac thought she heard it. In fact, she was certain she heard it. It was gurgling and boiling. *What is that?* Mac wondered. *Oh my gosh,* she thought, suddenly embarrassed. *It's my stomach!* Cheese gave her a funny look. Mac was hungry. She should have eaten Daphne's leftover blueberry pancakes. Now she was beyond hungry. She was starving and had no idea when the third graders got to eat lunch. Oh, just the thought of her dad's warm, fresh blueberry pancakes made her mouth water! She grew hungrier and more distracted by the minute. Her mind wandered back to breakfast. *I wonder if Dad cleaned the kitchen?* Mac thought. Somehow, she could picture her mother cleaning the stove, huffing and puffing the whole time. But where was her dad? Mac squinted her eyes, as she tried to see her parents in her mind. Yup, there they were. Bickering.

And then it happened again. That noise. That distinct, grumbling noise. It was even louder this time and Mac became doubly embarrassed when Randy turned around and laughed. And then triply embarrassed when Alison gave her a dirty look.

Even Lanie Kaplan, who has barely spoken out loud since first grade, stretched her neck around, scrunched up her face and said, "Who keeps making that noise?"

Mrs. Kearny gave all the children a Please-Be-Quiet Look. "I know it is the first day, and you have had an entire summer to play, and stay up late, and get out of the routine of school, but please, try to pay attention. By the way, I will walk you down to lunch right after this chapter," She said with a quick wink to Mac. "I know you can all make it. Remember, you're third graders now."

Then it happened again. Mac's stomach.

It was even louder and more grumbly than the previous two times. Mac had no choice but to laugh. She poked Charise in the ribs, ready to tell her some funny joke about her hunger. Instead, Cheese used her eyes to talk to Mac. Her eyes said: *Be quiet! Mrs. Kearny is serious.* At least that's what Mac thought Charise's eyes said. And so she did the best she could. She giggled here and there while trying to pay attention to the story and her stomach and her parents in the kitchen. *Fainting from hunger would be a huge mistake*, Mac thought. *I should say something. I should get something to eat. I need to eat. I wonder what dad packed me for lunch? I'm not going to make it. I, I, I—*

Finally, Mrs. Kearny said, "This is a good place to stop for today."

"You're a great out-loud reader," Chris

Collins said. "I like how you do the different voices."

Mrs. Kearny smiled a great, big smile and saluted Chris with a tiny two-fingered salute. Chris was so pleased with himself he threw his shoulders back and sat up so straight it looked as if he grew two inches.

"Tomorrow, to celebrate the second day of school, and the upcoming weekend, all at the same time, we will have a special guest reader. So, you will need to be on your extra-special guest behavior. Okay kids, walk to your desks. Pick up your lunches, and stand in a single file line. When you are ready, I will walk you to lunch."

She did it. Mac made it to lunch, talking stomach and all! She got her lunch and stood in line with her class. Her stomach growled and rumbled so loudly, even Mrs. Kearny had to say something this time. "Mac, perhaps you need a bigger breakfast," she said. The whole class laughed. Mac nodded and clenched her teeth tightly to prevent herself from saying anything funny because she knew if she did, she would be the one to get in trouble. The worst kind of trouble—the kind that included a forever grounding and that horrible look from her parents. The exact kind of trouble she was working so hard to avoid. *No more mistakes*, Mac reminded herself. Mac threw her shoulders back and stood in line with her classmates, proud that even her stomach growling didn't spoil her mission.

SIX

"Who do you think tomorrow's guest reader will be?" Mac asked Cheese, as she took a big bite of her sandwich.

"I know who it won't be," Randy chimed in. "It won't be the President of the United States. Or the First Lady either. I heard the news this morning before school and they are in Japan."

"Um, Randy," Alison said, "I have a feeling it wouldn't have been either of those people even if they were at the White House. And what are you eating anyway? It looks so—"

"Wrong," Mac said.

Alison didn't like agreeing with Mackenzie Goode, but Randy's lunch did look wrong. "Yes. Wrong," said Alison.

"Liverwurst, peanut butter and pickles. It's my favorite," he said with a piece of a Gherkin pickle hanging from his mouth. "And it could too be the First Lady. I saw how she likes to visit schools and read to the kids. We're kids. We're a nice school. Why not?"

"Why not?" said Mac. "Because she heard what you eat for lunch and left for

Japan before she had to see or smell it. That's why not."

The kids at the lunch table all laughed. Including Alison.

"So what kind of gourmet food are you eating Miss Eight Cowlick? Your lunch looks worse than mine," Randy shot back.

"Mine is a Goode delicacy. Cream cheese, cucumber, and alfalfa sprouts on a whole wheat wrap. Healthy and delicious."

"Maybe if you're a rabbit," Randy said.

Mackenzie was happy to see Randy's joke got a smaller laugh than hers.

"Nobody cares about your dumb lunches," Alison said, completely unhappy she wasn't the center of attention. "Here is what you should care about. I know who the mystery reader is."

"How? I mean who?" said Charise

nodding her head in slow motion, as if she knew everything. This time Mac had no idea what Cheese was trying to tell her, so Mac answered Cheese by furrowing her eyebrows.

"I'm not going to tell you," Alison said.

"If you're not going to tell us, why did you even bring it up?" Mac said. Cheese gave her another look and this time Mackenzie knew exactly what her best friend was saying.

"How badly do you want to know?" Alison said, twirling her perfectly long, straight, black, silky hair around her finger.

"You have no idea who the mystery reader is, do you?" Mac said.

Cheese grinned, slow and wide, adding a nod for extra effect.

Mac loved how she could read Cheese's

mind.

"I'll give you my chocolate chip cookies if you tell us," Randy said. "They're homemade, too."

"Randy, she doesn't know! She's just lying!" Mac said. "But I'll take a cookie." Mac reached across the table to grab one of Randy's mom's deliciously famous cookies.

"Do you know who the mystery reader is?" Randy said to Mac.

"No."

"So no cookie for you. Here, Alison. Take a cookie," Randy said. "Now will you tell me who tomorrow's guest is?"

Alison took the cookie and gave both Mac and Cheese her best Nah-Nah-I-Told-You-So look, before skipping over to Randy's side of the table and whispering in his ear.

Randy's eyes got big. Big with a capital B.

"Do you think they really know who the reader is?" Mac asked Cheese. "What if it is someone really famous? Could it be the First Lady? What if I make a stupid joke in front of the First Lady of the United States of America? What if my cowlicks are worse tomorrow than today?"

"I told you with my eyes," Cheese said. "Alison has no better idea than we do about who the reader will be. She's just trying to show off. Don't pay any attention to her. And you have that headband from France! Your hair will be perfect no matter who is reading."

"You think?"

"I know. Listen, I'll come over to your house after school today. We can work on your hair and we can practice using our eyes to talk."

"*Parfait!*" Mac said, using the French word Charise taught her.

"Okay, 3K lunch is over, time to return to our class," Mrs. Kearny said. Cheese nodded at Mac. The kids packed up their garbage and tossed it in the large can on their way back to an afternoon of learning. Mac, whose stomach was no longer rumbling, couldn't wait to practice her looks with Cheese. But still, she couldn't help but wonder whom tomorrow's mystery reader would be and if Randy and Alison really knew something she didn't.

SEVEN

"Hi, Mom! We're home!" Mackenzie shouted as she entered the front door after school.

"Hey Mac! Hey Daph. I'm in the kitchen. I'm slicing up a snack for you. Dad made zucchini bread this morning. *After* I cleaned up the pancake mess, I might add," Mom said.

"Ha! I was thinking about that! But it's actually me and Charise," Mac shouted.

"Charise and I."

"That's what I said," Mac said, rolling her eyes at Charise.

"Charise, dear. How was your summer? Did you all enjoy visiting with your grand-mère Charbonneau?

"Yup! And, she told me my French improved—in only three weeks."

"Yeah," Mac said. "She's even teaching me new words, like *parfait*."

"Wonderful, Cheese. Keep up the good work. And keep teaching Mac, too," Mom said, smiling at her youngest daughter. "By the way, where's your sister?"

"I don't know. Remember, we're on different busses now," Mac said.

"I just thought you'd see each other at

the bus stop and walk up the hill together. Come. Now, tell me about your day—both of you."

Each girl sat at the table and put two slices of the zucchini bread on their plates. Mom slid herself into the seat next to Mackenzie, grabbed a piece of the bread, and joined the girls for a snack.

Mackenzie took a big bite of the bread and watched Charise do the same.

"This is delicious," Charise said.

"It's Mr. Goode's famous recipe," Mom said. "He calls it Zany Zucchini Bread. Now if that man could just learn to clean up after himself" Mom said, rolling her eyes.

"Then what? You'd marry him?" Mac laughed, her mouth filled with food.

"Stop talking with your mouth full."

"But Mom, how can I tell you about my day and eat my snack at the same time. Don't you want to know everything?" Mackenzie continued without waiting for an answer from her mother. "It was a pretty good first day," Mac said, remembering her grumbling stomach, pleased it didn't ruin her no-mistakes promise. "Our classroom is great!" she continued.

Charise nodded in agreement while Mackenzie told her mother all about the four stations and the cool posters.

"And remember how Daphne told me Mrs. Kearny would salute us all? Well, she did. Each and every one of us. It's kind of goofy. But she doesn't wear a uniform and she is reading us this cool book. What was it called again, Cheese? And she says a guest is coming to our class tomorrow. And—"

Mac didn't get a chance to finish her sentence and Charise didn't get a chance to answer Mac's question before Mac's tornado of a sister entered the house screaming.

"I just had the *worst* day of my whole entire life," Daphne said from the hall. "Did you hear me? Worst!"

Mom, Mackenzie, and Charise just sat in silence.

"Hello! Anybody home? I'm in a crisis, here!"

"In the kitchen. Daph," Mom said.

"Ugh. My teachers are all so hard. I have homework in every subject. I am not in one class with Cynthia, but in every class with Blake Briar. *Blake Briar*. And tell me she doesn't think she is *all that*. She is the meanest girl I have ever laid eyes on. In fact, today she told me—"

"Daphne, dear. Take a breath," Mom said.

Daphne did not listen to her mother but instead continued ranting and raging on about her day.

"She told me I would never be cheerleading captain. She told me she would make sure that she, Blake Briar, would be captain. And then, she told me she didn't even want me on the squad. Can you believe that? I practically started the squad. Well, Cynthia and I did, anyway. She can't—Mackenzie Goode! Your hair!" Daphne screamed.

"What?" Mac said reaching for her head, afraid her hair was on fire or something.

"It actually looks good. What in the world did you do? Oh, hi Cheese," Daphne said, finally noticing exactly who was sitting at the table.

A big smile spread across Mackenzie's face. "This is a headband from France. Charise gave it to me. Everyone wears them in Paris, right Cheese?"

"*Mai oui, mon ami*," Cheese said, giving Mac a wink.

"And, it really keeps all eight cowlicks in place," Mac added.

"Yes. Yes it does," Daphne said. "And did I mention I have homework in every single subject? I have no idea how I am going to complete all this work and practice my cheers! Tryouts begin tomorrow. Why in the world would they start tryouts on a Friday? Don't you think they would give us the weekend to—"

It was during this particular part of Daphne's rant that Mac and Cheese snuck out. Mom and Daphne didn't even notice. Or, if they did, they chose not to say anything. The girls sat at the top of the steps, halfway between the kitchen and Mac's room.

"Eighth grade sounds pretty hard," Charise said.

"Oh, but my sister does love the drama! Let's keep listening to her tantrum and practice using our eyes to talk," Mac said.

"Good idea. I'll start," Charise said. "What am I saying?"

Charise made one eyebrow go up and let the other one stay down. And then, she kind of turned her mouth down. Mac stared at her face, trying to determine what it meant.

"You're wondering if you will be able to survive eighth grade."

"That is exactly correct! Mackenzie Goode, you really can read my mind."

"Okay, my turn. What am I saying?" Mackenzie said. Her face was kind of blank, and her eyes stuck in a glazed, far away stare. Charise's mouth twisted into a small knowing grin.

"You're wondering if Alison and Randy really know who tomorrow's mystery reader is."

"You are a Genius with a capital G! That is exactly what I was saying. How about now?" Mac squeezed her eyes shut so tightly the rest of her face looked like a prune.

"You're wondering if you will be able to make it through third grade without making one mistake."

"Nope. I was thinking I'm bored of hearing Daphne go on and on and on about her dumb day. But now that you mention it, I am pretty worried about that. C'mon. To my room," Mac said. "Let's make all the bobblehead dolls move at the same time."

EIGHT

It was hard for the kids of 3K to sit still on Friday, the second day of school. They all knew there was a "guest" coming to their classroom. Mac was worried Alison and Randy knew something she didn't, and Alison and Randy were busy making sure she continued to feel that way. They smiled and nodded their heads at one another all morning. Mackenzie couldn't help but wonder if Alison and Randy practiced using their eyes to talk, too.

"Okay, 3K," Mrs. Kearny said, giving all her students a great big sweeping salute. "Let's finish working on our summer paragraphs. If you feel like you are nearly finished, come up to my desk and we can begin the process of editing."

Mac perched up high in her seat and glanced up to Alison's paper. It was nearly completely filled. *Wrong.* And it was single spaced, too. *Double wrong.* She looked over at Charise who was busy writing. Her paper was nearly halfway filled. Then, she looked down at her own paper. All that was written on it was *"My Summer" by Mackenzie Goode.* Mackenzie could barely remember what she did over the summer.

But, thanks to her headband from France, she was having a good hair day. And, thanks to all the practicing she did with Charise, she was pretty sure they could talk using their eyes. And, thanks to the joke book Mrs. Kearny let her borrow, she knew ten new jokes by heart. Mackenzie Goode was excited to hear more from *Nothing is Impossible* and anxious to discover whom the guest reader would be. But as for summer? How could she possibly concentrate on summer? It was just a memory.

All Mackenzie could focus on was today. Now. This moment. She watched students like Lanie and Tyler go up to Mrs. Kearny's desk. She watched Randy write and erase. Write and erase. But mostly, she played with her hair and watched the clock tic, tic, tic away. *Time never flies when you need it to,* Mackenzie thought. *If this were gym class, it would already be over.*

"Okay, class. Please put your papers away," Mrs. Kearny said. "We will complete these paragraphs early next week and post them outside our classrooms so your parents can read them when they visit on Back to School Night. So far, they are all wonderful. After your papers are away and your desks are clean, join me on the red carpet."

Phew! Mackenzie thought. *I made it.*

She checked on Randy. His eyes got big and wide. Alison smiled a huge smile. Mac and Cheese just looked at each other. Even though neither girl really thought the First Lady would be their guest, it was still, they both imagined, a possibility. Unlikely, but hey, you never knew. Randy and Alison sure were excited about something.

Mac sat in the back. Again, she was knee to knee with Charise. Just the way she liked it. Mrs. Kearny sat in her chair in front of the class.

"Okay, kids, today we will continue on our literary journey, reading *Nothing is Impossible*. Where did we leave off yesterday?"

Alison was the first to shoot her hand up.

"Okay, Allison," Mrs. Kearny said. "You can refresh our memories."

Allison stood up and turned to face the class. Mac rolled her eyes at Charise who rolled her own eyes right back. Mac just knew they were both thinking the very same thing. *Wrong*.

"Well, it's kind of not fair, but I read this book over the summer," Alison said. "By myself," she added with a huge grin. "But yesterday we met Trace, this farm girl. She wants to grow the biggest pumpkin in the county and win the pumpkin contest at the fair. Oh, and she wears these gross overalls every day. Anyway, nobody thinks she can win because she is only seven years old. Not even her mom, who wants her to bake pies instead. And her best friend is a horse named Charlie. Oh, and—"

"Nice refresher, Alison." Mrs. Kearny stopped Alison from continuing. "Thank you. You may sit down. I have to say, I like Trace's overalls. I think wearing overalls every day gives her a sense of routine and comfort."

Mackenzie's eyes grew big and she tried to tell Charise she liked Trace's overalls, too. She wondered if Charise knew what she was saying. For a moment, she forgot to pay attention to Mrs. Kearny, who was still talking

"So, my friends, as I promised, we have a guest reader today."

The children were on their knees, anxious to find out who the mystery reader was. "Visiting our class for the first time is—"

"Teen pop star, Baylor Fast," Alison said, before Mrs. Kearny could even finish her sentence. Even worse than just calling out, Alison jumped up and shouted the name. "Baylor Fast!"

"Baylor Fast?" Mrs. Kearny said, using a voice that screamed *no way*! "Why in the world would you think our guest reader is Baylor Fast?" Mrs. Kearny's eyebrows looked like two sideways question marks. Mac wondered if Mrs. Kearny was good at talking with her eyes, too.

Alison turned bright red. And if eyes could really talk, Randy's eyes were saying the meanest things about Alison. She had him convinced Baylor Fast was coming to school! *Baylor Fast! That's hysterical,* Mackenzie thought. *Note to self: Give Randy my Baylor Fast bobblehead doll. That will make him feel better.* Because Randy was mad. Mad with a capital M. Mackenzie couldn't control herself. She broke out in a fit of laughter.

"Well, I read in my magazine how she was born here. And sometimes she likes to visit. And, you know she is giving a concert in the city tonight. So I sort of put two and two together," said Alison.

"And made five!" shouted Mac. Pleased with the timing of her joke, which got a big laugh from her classmates.

"And I was dumb enough to waste one of my mother's extra spectacular cookies on you," Randy said.

Mac just couldn't stop laughing. She kept giving Charise an elbow to the ribs. Charise thought it was funny, all right, but not nearly as funny as Mac found it.

"Settle down, children. What I was going to say was—visiting our class for the first time is—"

Mac wasn't certain, but she thought Mrs. Kearny paused a bit too long there, waiting for another silly outburst.

". . . your school principal, Mr.

Donatello," Mrs. Kearny said.

And with that, Mr. Donatello, who must have heard everything from the hallway, walked into room 3K. "I'm no Baylor Fast, but I do love a good book," he said with a chuckle.

Mac jabbed Cheese in the ribs again and whispered ever so quietly, "I almost feel bad for Alison. Look how mad Randy is. But there is good news! My stomach isn't growling today. I doubled up on breakfast."

"I am happy for you and your stomach," Charise whispered back. "Now be quiet. Mr. Donatello is here."

"Well," Mr. Donatello said, taking the seat previously occupied by Mrs. Kearny, I am sorry to disappoint you, but let's check out chapter two of this fine book."

And then, Mr. Donatello began to read. His voices were not nearly as good as Mrs. Kearny's. His Charlie voice was no different from his Trace voice, which was no different from his mom voice. He kind of sounded the same the whole time. Instead of getting involved, Mackenzie was tuning out. She let her mind wander. She got so far away eventually she didn't even hear Mr. Donatello's voice. All she heard was blah, blah, blah.

"Cheese," she said, nudging her friend with her knee. "I have a song for you,"

"Later," Cheese said. "Pay attention, now."

"But it's good," Mackenzie said.

"Pay attention, Mac," Cheese said, using the Red-Flag-Red-Flag-You-Are-About-to-Make-a-Mistake look they practiced last night.

Mackenzie didn't notice Charise using her eyes talk.

"It goes like this . . ." Mackenzie said.

I wasn't born when I met you
And yet we were meant to
Best friends be
We stick together—it's you and me"

"Mac, be quiet. Look, Mrs. Kearny is watching you," Charise said.

Mac looked up and it was true. Mrs. Kearny was giving her a very bad look. It was a Be-Quiet-Now look. She was pretty good at using her eyes to talk. But what Mac was not good at was listening. She was writing a song. She was on a roll. And then, Mac glanced over the room and saw a big, pickle-tooth grin on Randy's face. His smile was practically insisting Mac continue.

"Listen, Cheese, there's more," Mac said. Cheese tried really hard to talk to Mac with her eyes. She begged. She pleaded. But Mac was too far gone to listen. She continued to serenade Charise.

It was hard for Charise to hear Mac's song and *Nothing is Impossible* and use her eyes to tell Mac to STOP all at the same time. This day was going very badly, but Mac's song was kind of funny. Even Charise had to smile at it. But it was a Very with a capital V tiny smile.

Mrs. Kearny was making her eyes really narrow and when she did, her lips practically disappeared. "There is smoke coming out of her ears," Charise whispered under her breath but Mackenzie didn't hear Charise. And she wouldn't have stopped anyway.

"Not another verse," Cheese continued to talk under her breath. "Stop singing Mackenzie!" It was no use.

Mr. Donatello was not at all aware of the commotion. He kept reading and reading in his boring, same-same voice. And Mrs. Kearny was making new and even more awful mad faces at Mackenzie.

"Shhhhh," Mrs. Kearny said, staring directly at Mackenzie. Mrs. Kearny would have sent Mackenzie to the principal's office but the problem was, the principal wasn't in his office. He was in Mrs. Kearny's class.

"My song's almost done," Mackenzie whispered. Charise gave up trying to stop her best friend, because clearly there was no stopping her.

Mackenzie smiled when her song was finished. "What do you think, Cheese?"

"I think you are in Big with a capital B trouble," Charise said.

Mackenzie raised her eyebrows in disbelief and tilted her head. "Why?"

"Well, thank you for allowing me to read to you," Mr. Donatello said. "I hope I can come back and do it again."

"We would love that," Mrs. Kearny said, clapping wildly, getting the children to clap along with her. "What do we say, children?"

"Thank you Mr. Donatello," they all said together. Except for Mac, who instead whispered to Cheese, "I hope he doesn't read to us ever, ever again."

As soon as Mr. Donatello left the room, Mrs. Kearny shut the door.

"I am so disappointed," she said. Her face was huffy and red. "Mackenzie Goode, I will see you after school. Now return to your desks, children. Get your lunches and I will walk you down to the cafeteria."

Mackenzie suddenly felt sick to her stomach. *Oh, what have I done?* She wondered. *And after trying so hard, too! This is just wrong!* Mackenzie knew she made a very big mistake and whatever came next was going to be Awful with a capital A.

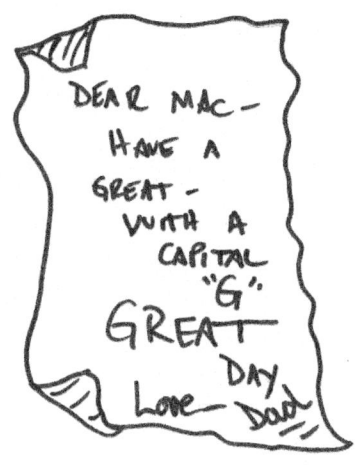

NINE

"I can't eat," Mackenzie said. "Anyone want my lunch?"

"You are in serious trouble!" Randy said. "And I mean *serious*! What do you have to eat anyway?"

"Oh, I don't know. Cucumber wrap, zucchini bread, apple," Mac said with no energy, just dumping the contents of her lunch sack on the table. Out with her lunch spilled a note written from her dad.

Dear Mac,

Have a Great—with a capital "G" GREAT day!

Love,

Dad

Mackenzie sighed after reading the note then shoved it in her pocket.

"Pass it over here," Randy said. "I'll eat it. What are you going to do, Mackenzie?"

"Yeah, what are you going to do?" Alison chimed in. "I would hate to be you right now. Actually, I would hate to be you on any day, but today I think it would be worse."

"I guess I'll go see Mrs. Kearny after school. And you're in trouble, too, you know," Mackenzie said to Alison. "You totally lied to Randy."

"I didn't lie, I just got the facts wrong. But I would rather have Randy mad at me than Mrs. Kearny. I mean look at him," Alison said.

And there was Randy, shoving different pieces of all the lunch foods in his mouth at the same time. *Wrong*, Mac thought.

"I know exactly what Mackenzie will do," Charise said.

Mackenzie's eyes got a touch brighter. Leave it to a best friend to figure stuff out.

"She is going to sit up a bit straighter, smile a bit brighter and hold her head high."

Mackenzie followed right along as Charise spoke.

"She is going to admit she made a

mistake."

"I did. I made a very big mistake, guys," Mac said.

"Parfait," Cherise whispered to Mac, before continuing in her regular voice.

"And then she is going back to 3K for an afternoon of school. And we are all, and I mean all," and with that, Charise stared at Alison, "going to stand by her. Then, after last period, which is gym, Mackenzie will go to her locker, get her things for the weekend and I will walk her to 3K, where she will meet with Mrs. Kearny. She will apologize. And then she will start fresh."

Mackenzie kind of liked the plan. When Charise put it like that, the whole event wasn't so overwhelming.

"But none of this will happen until Mac sings us the song," Charise said.

"Huh?" Mac said.

"The song you made up. It's good, you know. What I heard of it anyway. You just tried it out at the wrong time. This is a better time for it. So, go ahead. Sing," Cheese said.

A big grin spread across Mackenzie's face. And she sang:

"I wasn't born when I met you
And yet we were meant to
Best friends be
We stick together—it's you and me

We go together like mac and cheese
It's the tastiest—If you please
Try to make it with Cheddar and Swiss
The dish is delish
The mac is the Ace
And the cheese takes first place

Mackenzie Goode Makes a Mistake

You always fix my hair
And all our friends are quite aware
That we are best friends
Just like bookends

We go together like mac and cheese
It's the tastiest — If you please
Try to make it with Cheddar and Swiss
The dish is delish
The mac is the Ace
And the cheese takes first place"

By the end of lunch, everyone was singing Mackenzie's song. Mackenzie couldn't help but smile and wonder how a song so right could have turned out all *wrong*. For the moment anyway, thanks to Charise, her stomachache was gone. She grabbed the last slice of zucchini bread, the one Randy hadn't touched yet, and shoved it in her mouth. That should keep the growling away, she thought.

"Thanks, Charise," Mackenzie whispered to her friend.

Charise smiled and used her eyes to say *anytime.*

TEN

With great fear and doubt and tons of butterflies in her stomach, Mackenzie entered Mrs. Kearny's room. It was 3:00 p.m., the time when kids who were *not* in trouble were busy with after-school activities and play dates and all things fun! And, the time when kids who *were* in trouble were stuck in an empty school. The shades were drawn. The room was dark. The fantastic reading, writing, science, and math stations were lifeless. The room, which seemed to fit her class perfectly during the day, appeared too cold and too large right now. Mac's stomach growled, but she was certain it was the butterflies talking and not hunger. Behind a brown, wooden teacher desk sat Mrs. Kearny. She looked like Captain Kearny all right, steering a large Navy ship, and Mackenzie was going to have to "walk the plank."

"Um—Cap—I mean, Mrs. Kearny?"

"Come closer, Mackenzie," Mrs. Kearny said.

Mackenzie walked three steps toward the desk. She could feel the sweat starting to bead up on her forehead. And oh boy, did her stomach hurt.

"Mackenzie, your behavior today was rude, repugnant, and repulsive," Mrs. Kearny said.

"I know. I'm sorry," Mackenzie said, not at all certain what two of those three words even meant, except for Big, Fat, Trouble. "I will—"

"I am talking right now. I have never in my entire teaching career seen such a poor display of behavior. I stared at you. I shhh'd you. And still, you didn't stop talking. I don't know what your parents are teaching you at home, but clearly, manners isn't part of the program."

"I—" Mackenzie tried to talk again.

"I said I'm talking right now, Mackenzie. Monday is only the third day of school. I will not tolerate this behavior for an entire year. You will stay after school with me all next week and file papers, erase the boards, and think about how you can change your behavior."

"Yes, Mrs. Kearny," Mackenzie said, her eyes filling up with tears. Mackenzie turned around and started to leave 3K, hoping she could get outside before her tears started falling.

"And Mackenzie, one more thing—if you were *my* daughter, you would be grounded for life."

"Yes, Mrs. Kearny," Mackenzie whispered. She ran out of the classroom and into the arms of Charise, who was waiting right outside the door for her best friend.

Mackenzie sobbed that uncontrollable sob. The one where you can't catch your breath. "I can't tell my parents," Mackenzie said between gasps of air. "They will never forgive me," she said, pulling out the note her dad put in her lunch and shoving it into Charise's face to read. "They will ground me for life—"

"Just read this note. They love you, Mac."

"No, Charise, they used to love me. They loved the yesterday me. They will not love the today me. The today me is all wrong."

"They will forgive you. C'mon. Let's go home," Charise said. "Everything will be okay." Charise gave Mackenzie a pat on the arm.

Mackenzie flinched. She wasn't so sure.

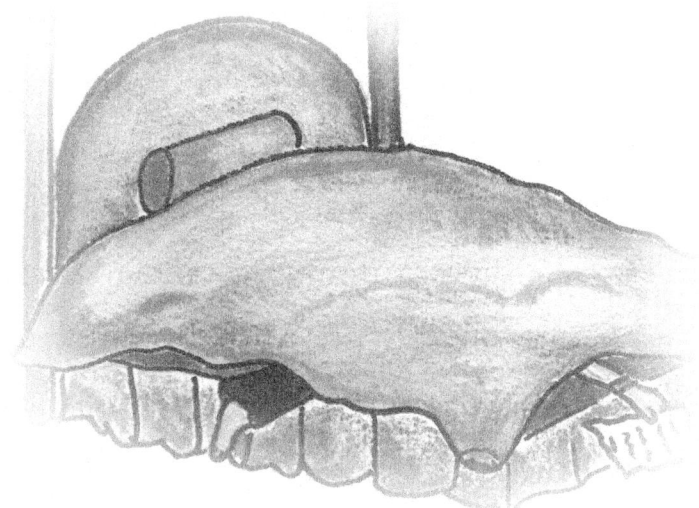

ELEVEN

"I'm home," Mackenzie said, not waiting for any response, but deciding instead to run up to her room before she had to face her mother.

"Mac? How was your day? Are you hungry? Do you want a snack? Is Charise with you?" Mom said.

"Fine. No, no, and no," Mac shouted from her room, remembering to respond to each question. In her room, Mackenzie was confronted by her bobblehead collection, all twenty-three of them. And even the site of the Three Stooges didn't make her smile.

"Why are you running to your room so fast? Come on down," Mom shouted up the steps, in the direction of Mackenzie's room.

"Later," Mac said. "I just want to chill out first."

"Okay," Mom paused a moment and put her hand to her head. "I'll be in my office," she added, her voice cracking and high pitched, like she was asking a question and not making a statement. Before she had a chance to dwell on Mackenzie, Daphne raced through the door.

"Daph? Why are you home? I thought

you had tryouts after school," Mom said.

"Coach got smart and decided to give us the weekend to practice. Even Blake Briar was happy. Go figure," Daphne said. "Mac home?"

"Yes, but she went straight to her room."

"Without eating?" Daphne raised her eyebrows.

"I know. I thought it was strange too." Mom's voice was still squeaky.

"I have a feeling something's up with that child," Daphne said.

"What do you mean?" Mom tugged at her hair.

"I found this book in the driveway." Daphne shoved the book, *1001 Jokes and How to Tell Them*, under her mother's nose. "It has to be Mac's."

"Yeah, but—"

"Let's piece this together. If she were well, she would guard a book like this with her life."

Mom nodded in agreement.

"And she would eat lots and lots of food," Daphne added.

"And she would be with Charise," Mom chimed in.

"Or waiting for me. Getting ready to shove me in the bathroom, or something. I knew something was up with that little twerp the minute I saw this book. I just knew it."

"Sounds like you could be right. I'll go check on her." Mom cupped her ear and tilted her head, as if she had heard a noise upstairs.

It was Mackenzie. She had popped out

of her room and sat at the top of the stairs to eavesdrop on her mom and sister's conversation. Mackenzie started to sweat at the prospect of coming clean. She raced back to her room and hid under her covers, her heart nearly pounding out of her chest.

"No way. I'm going in myself," Daphne said, moving her arms as if she were about to begin a cheer. "And I'm going to get to the bottom of it."

"Please be gentle, Daph." Mom said.

"Aren't I always?" Daphne said.

"Um, no."

Daphne didn't wait for her mother's response. She just flew up the stairs and banged on Mac's door.

"I'm resting," Mac said.

"It's me. Daphne."

"Go away. I want to be alone."

Daphne refused to be denied. She barged in Mac's room and found her sister huddled in her bed, completely covered by her comforter. Not even one of her eight cowlicks was sticking out. "Look, I found this." Daphne said.

"What?" Mackenzie said.

"Your joke book."

"Keep it. Burn it. I don't care. I'm not telling jokes anymore," Mackenzie said.

"Yeah, right! You not telling a joke is like me not being dramatic. Never going to happen, my friend," Daphne said.

Daphne couldn't see it, but Mac did crack the tiniest of smiles deep under all her covers.

"We can do this the easy way, or the hard way," Daphne said. "But I am *not* leaving this room until you tell me what happened." Then, she dropped the joke book on Mac's bed.

"Leave me alone. My time on earth is short and I don't want to spend my last hours with you," Mackenzie said.

"That's a pretty good line," Daphne said. "Your timing was perfect. I'll have to use it sometime."

Still under the covers, Mac smiled again.

"Okay Little Miss Eight Cowlicks, I invented the word drama. This is me. Daphne? Remember? Just tell me what happened. For the love of all these ridiculous bobblehead dolls, tell me."

Mackenzie waited a few seconds and then decided it might be good to tell someone in her family. "Well, I got in trouble at school. Big with a capital B trouble. And I'm afraid to tell mom, because when I do, I will be grounded for life. And she will hate me. And she will give me that look. That totally disappointed look. And forget about Dad, after he wrote me this note and all." Mackenzie poked her hand out from under the covers to show her sister the note.

"I wouldn't blame him if he never wrote me another note. Or made me another lunch. Or even talked to me. Ever again," Mac said.

"Listen, Mackenzie, this sounds pretty serious. I'm going to get Mom. But before I do, let me tell you there is no problem Mom or Dad can't help solve. And I've given them some pretty tough ones, too. Stop being so, well, dramatic. They love you and even though it pains me to admit it, so do I. So sit up, and wait right here. Mom can help fix anything."

TWELVE

"Mac," Mom knocked gently on the door. "May I come in?"

"If you really want to," Mac said.

Mac was sitting straight up in her bed, just like her sister told her to do. Her hair was even more messy than usual and her eyes were puffy and red from so much crying.

"From the looks of it, I'm guessing you had a pretty bad day. Do you want to tell me about it?"

"No."

"How about if I tell you I want to hear about it. Does that make a difference?"

It did. Mac spilled everything. She told her mom neither the First Lady nor Baylor Fast were the guest readers, but her principal was. She told her mom about *Nothing is Impossible* with Trace and Charlie and growing the pumpkin. And how, without Mrs. Kearny reading, and all her fantastic voices, it was totally boring. She told her mom how she didn't pay attention even though Charise tried to talk to her with her eyes and how Mrs. Kearny *really* tried to talk to her with her eyes. And how she made up that dumb song and sang it to Cheese the whole time Mr. Donatello read. And how she had to stay after school and how dark the room was and how mean

Mrs. Kearny was and how she's had a sick stomach ever since and hasn't been able to stop crying. And she kept talking and talking until her mom forced her to take a breath.

"And the worst part is—" Mackenzie sobbed. "The worst part is, I'm not so, Mom."

"I'm not following you, Mackenzie."

"I'm *not so!*"

"Not so?"

"I'm NOT SO GOODE."

"Aw, honey, you're a good Goode, not a bad Goode. Here's how I know. You're my Goode kid who made a mistake."

"But I wasn't supposed to make any more mistakes in the third grade."

"What do you mean?" Mom said, her eyes wide with curiosity.

"Well, after second grade when I was grounded for life for calling out in class, I saw something in yours and Daddy's eyes. Something I never wanted to see again."

Mom didn't say a word, but her eyes said *tell me*.

Mac waited for what felt like forever. Mom kept her eyes locked on Mac.

"Disappointment," Mac finally said, her voice no louder than a whisper.

Mom shook her head in agreement, paused for a moment and then spoke. "Mackenzie, when I was a little girl, I had a favorite record."

"Mom!"

"Just listen, honey. My Aunt Jody gave it to me. It was a Sesame Street album. And I thought it was *perfect*. I would put it on my little portable turntable and listen to it over and over again."

"Mom!"

"I'm getting there, Mac. Promise. Big Bird sang my favorite song. And to this day, I still remember the lyrics. It goes like this:

Oh everyone makes mistakes.

Oh, yes they do.

Your sister and your brother and your dad and mother, too;

Big people, small people, matter of fact, all people!

Everyone makes mistakes, so why can't you?

"Really?"

"Really."

"Do you still make mistakes, Mom?"

"Of course I do. And when you make

mistakes, it is likely a few people will be disappointed along the way. I have made mistakes that disappointed my mom.

"*You* disappointed *Grandma*?" Mac gasped at the thought.

"Of course. And she disappointed her mom. But I don't want you to confuse disappointment with love."

Mackenzie scrunched her nose in confusion.

"Grandma's mom always loved her and Grandma always loved me, disappointments and all. And *I* will always love *you*. Daddy will, too."

Mac nodded.

"The thing about mistakes is that we have to learn from them so we don't make the same ones over and over again. For example, now that I'm thirty-seven, I wouldn't make the mistake you made today. I already made that one, back when I was your age. And here's something else important: we have to remember to apologize whenever we make a mistake."

"But how, I mean who, I mean—"

"I think the person you really need to apologize to is Mr. Donatello. And you can start by writing him a note." Mom walked over the Mackenzie's desk and got a pencil and a piece of paper. "I see you already have a book to lean on," Mom said, nodding at the joke book on Mackenzie's bed.

Mackenzie picked up the book. She decided it was okay to lean on, as long as she didn't open it. Jokes always got her in trouble.

"What should I say?"

"Whatever is in your heart. That is always the best kind of apology."

"And how about Mrs. Kearny? How am I ever going to face her again? She's going to hate me for the rest of the year."

"Hate is a strong word, Mac. She was disappointed, but truthfully, it sounds like she was having a pretty bad day, too. And perhaps, the way she talked to you was one of those grown up mistakes and—"

Dad burst into Mackenzie's room. "Daph said Mackenzie has the third grade flu? Are you okay Mac?" Dad said, looking at Mom for some sort of sign that everything was okay. Between Mom and Mackenzie, they shared the whole story.

After all the words spilled out, Mom and Dad looked at each other and talked using only their eyes. *I wish I knew what they were saying*, Mackenzie thought.

"Well, guess what Little Miss Eight Cowlicks? After all that information, you know what I am most curious about? The song! I want to hear the song! Sounds like you wrote a winner of a song, but shared it at the wrong time. You're biggest mistake was a lack of timing, my dear."

Then, Dad noticed the joke book on Mackenzie's bed. "All comedians need to learn the art of timing, Mac. I bet there is an entire chapter devoted to timing right there in that book of yours. Read it! And work on your timing, Mackenzie, but don't, for one second, stop writing songs or telling jokes! It's your gift."

"Am I punished?" Mac asked.

Mom looked at Dad and Dad looked at Mom. Mom spoke. "You already know how disrespectful your behavior was. And you are going to apologize for that behavior. We can see how sorry you are and how upset this entire day has made you. Under these circumstances, that seems to be just the right amount of punishment. We love you, Mackenzie Goode. Mistakes and all."

Mom and Dad left her alone and Mackenzie was certain she saw them talking with their eyes. *What am I going to write in this note,* she wondered. *Make it from the heart,* she remembered. She looked at her heart to see if there were any words in there. It was empty. *Wrong.*

THIRTEEN

It was Sunday night and Mackenzie was in her room. She just finished dinner and desert, steak and then father's secret oatmeal chocolate chip cookies. She could hear her mother cleaning up the mess, and making her motherly groaning noises the whole time. It felt good to get back to normal again. But she knew it wouldn't last. She had to face tomorrow, and just that single thought made her stomach do that flip-flop thing again.

She knew she wasn't hungry. No, it was that exact same sick feeling she had in Mrs. Kearny's dark, dark room. It was what Daphne called The Third Grade Flu. But Mackenzie preferred calling it: the I-have-to-apologize-tomorrow-and-I'm-scared-out-of-my-mind disease. Would it ever go away?

Just as she was wondering, the phone rang. She ran to pick it up. It was Charise. How did Charise know to call at that exact moment? Mac was relieved she did.

"Just checking in, Mac. And confirming tomorrow's plan,"

"Okay," Mac said, her voice filled with a big dose of scared.

"Relax, Mac. Tomorrow will pass, just

like today. You will see Mr. Donatello and Mrs. Kearny and you will, I promise, get to be able to enjoy third grade."

"I don't know," Mac said.

"You say I don't know, but I say I do know. Now listen. Your mom is driving you to school early, right?"

"Right."

"Well, my mom is going to drive me early, too. I'll meet you at the flagpole, okay? I'll walk with you to Mr. Donatello's office and I'll wait outside the room while you do your thing. If you get scared, you'll know I'm right there. You can do it, Mac."

"Hey," Mac said. "My stomach didn't flip-flop once, the whole time you were talking. Maybe I can do this," Mac said. She really wanted to believe it.

FOURTEEN

Mackenzie Goode tapped ever so lightly on Principal Donatello's door. Perhaps if he doesn't hear me, she thought, I won't have to go in. Charise knew exactly what Mackenzie was thinking.

"I'll be right here, Mac," Charise said. "You can do it."

"Come in," Mr. Donatello said.

Mackenzie entered. Slowly.

"Mackenzie Goode, what can I help you with this morning? Did you have a GOODE weekend? Get it? Goode?" And then he chuckled a smooth, easy chuckle that made Mackenzie's shoulders lower in relaxation.

Why was he being so nice? She didn't deserve nice.

"Well—" and she hesitated for a moment. "Well, I wanted to give you this," she said, pulling her note out of her backpack and handing it to her principal. "I was kind of, sort of, hoping, maybe you would read it now," she said.

"Well then, I will do just that." Mr. Donatello put on his glasses, opened the envelope using a fancy letter opener he had on his desk, and then began to read.

Dear Mr. Donatello

I am sorry. You were reading that really nice story to us and I wasn't paying attention. I was being rude and talking to my best friend when I shouldn't have been. I am trying really hard not to make any mistakes now that I am in third grade, but I guess I didn't do a good job of it. I will try harder from now on. I hope you can forgive me. And this note would look so much fancier if I could write in cursive. We are going to learn cursive this year. Maybe I can write you another note after I learn cursive.

Your friend (I hope),

Mackenzie Goode

Mr. Donatello took his glasses off and then looked right at Mackenzie. "This is a wonderful note, Mackenzie. How very grown up of you. I bet it wasn't easy to come in here this morning, but doing the right thing isn't always easy. I am very proud of you and yes, I do accept your apology. Remember, life isn't about not making any mistakes, but rather it is about learning from the mistakes we do make. Friend?" Mr. Donatello said, standing up and reaching out to shake Mackenzie's hand.

"Friend," she said reaching her hand out to shake back.

Then, as slowly as she entered Mr. Donatello's office is as fast as she scurried out. She found Charise waiting for her, just as promised.

"How was it?" Charise asked.

"Not bad at all! He was so nice," Mackenzie said. "He said I was very grown up. He said he was proud. And, he said we are friends. He also said we have to learn from our mistakes. Come to think of it, he sounds a lot like my parents," Mac said.

"They must learn all that at grown-up school," Charise said.

"I'm afraid my next stop won't be so easy," Mackenzie said as the two girls inched closer to 3K. "I hope the shades are opened today. It was so dark and scary in that room on Friday."

"Remember," Charise said. "I am right outside the door if you need me."

The door to 3K was wide open. Mackenzie spotted Mrs. Kearny sitting at her desk. She was also thankful to notice the blinds were, in fact, raised and the sun was shining in the room. *Phew*, Mac thought.

"Mrs. Kearny," Mackenzie said in a

voice so low it was begging Mrs. Kearny not to hear.

"Mackenzie," she said. "Please come in. Oh, dear, I wanted to talk to you today and I figured I would do so over lunch, but it is just brilliant you came in early. I must apologize, dear."

"What?" Mackenzie said, tugging at her ears, not certain she heard her teacher correctly.

"I must apologize to you."

"Wait. You're apologizing to me?"

"Yes, in fact, here is a little note I wrote to you. I would like for you to read it now, if that is okay.

Mackenzie took hold of the note and opened it. Boy, how she wished she had Mr. Donatello's fancy letter opener. The note said:

Dear Mackenzie,

I thought about what happened on Friday this whole entire weekend. Honestly, I have been sick about it. While it is true, I wasn't pleased with your behavior, I do believe I came on a little, shall we say, strong. I'm afraid I was having a bad day, and with much regret I took it out on you. And for that, Mackenzie, I am sorry.

I hope you accept my apology and we can work on a great third grade year together. You are a wonderful child with a spunky personality.

Your teacher,

Mrs. Kearny

"Oh, wow, Mrs. Kearny. That's a really nice note. And I'm sorry, too," Mackenzie said. "I accept your apology. You want to know why?"

"Indeed."

Mackenzie smiled, as she thought of her mom and that long, long story about Big Bird and Sesame Street. Finally, Mackenzie really, completely, and totally understood why her mother told her that story. "Well a long, long time ago, Big Bird—do you remember Big Bird, Mrs. Kearny?

"I do."

"Well, like I said, a really long time ago, he sang this song and it goes *everyone makes mistakes, so why can't you?*"

Mrs. Kearny laughed. It was a genuine one, too. Mac could tell.

"You know what, Mackenzie, now that you mention it, I do remember that song! And it *was* a long time ago. Maybe I can Google the lyrics and make a new poster for our classroom. What do you think?"

"I like that idea just fine," Mackenzie said.

"Well then, I'm glad all is A-OK," Mrs. Kearny said, giving Mackenzie a great big salute. Mackenzie was so thrilled to receive such a great big salute, she didn't for one second think a Captain Kearny salute was dumb. In fact, Mackenzie grinned a huge grin and saluted back.

"One more thing?" Mac said.

Mrs. Kearny smiled a smile that said *go ahead*.

"Does Trace grow the biggest pumpkin?"

"Well, I guess you'll just have to listen and see," Mrs. Kearny said, using the voice she made up for Charlie the horse. "Just remember, nothing is impossible."

Mac laughed out loud. Then she turned

on her heels and saw Cheese smiling at her in the doorway. Mac talked to Cheese without using any words and she knew, with complete certainty, they were saying the exact same thing . . . and it was all *parfait.*

We go together like mac and cheese
It's the tastiest — If you please
Try to make it with Cheddar and Swiss
The dish is delish
The mac is the Ace
And the cheese takes first place

SOME GOODE RECIPES

A Goode Lunch: Cream Cheese and Cucumber Wrap

1 whole wheat wrap
2 Tbsp cream cheese
1 cucumber; peeled and sliced (like discs)
1 bunch alfalfa sprouts
Salt and pepper to taste

Place open wrap on work surface; spread with 2 Tbsp cream cheese until cream cheese almost touches the edges.

Arrange cucumber circles on top of cream cheese (use as many as you like).

Top with a bunch of alfalfa sprouts.

Add a pinch of Sea Salt and fresh ground black pepper.

Fold the right and the left end of the wrap toward the center. Then roll it up (like you are rolling a piece of poster board) and cut the wrap in half.

Zany Zucchini Bread

1½ cup whole wheat flour

½ tsp baking soda

½ tsp baking powder

1 tsp cinnamon

½ tsp nutmeg

1 egg

1/3 cup vegetable oil

1/3 cup unsweetened applesauce

2 Tbsp fat free sour cream

¾ cup light brown sugar

2 tsp vanilla extract

2 cup grated zucchini

Heat oven to 325 F. Spray an 8-inch loaf pan with cooking spray. Set aside.

In large bowl mix together flour, baking soda, baking powder, cinnamon, and nutmeg.

In separate bowl, whisk together egg, oil, applesauce, sour cream, sugar, and vanilla.

Add flour mixture to egg mixture and stir until well combined.

Fold in zucchini then transfer to loaf pan. Bake until risen, golden brown and a toothpick inserted in the middle comes out clean, about 60 to 70 minutes.

Cool in pan for 30 minutes. Then, remove bread from pan and continue to cool on rack.

Dad's Secret Oatmeal Chocolate Chip Cookies

(not so secret anymore)

½ cup plus 6 Tbsp butter, softened

1 cup firmly packed light brown sugar

2 eggs

1 tsp vanilla

1 ¼ cup whole wheat flour

¼ cup ground flax seed

1 tsp baking soda

1 tsp ground cinnamon

3 cups oats

1 cup chocolate chips

Heat oven to 350 F. In large bowl, beat butter and sugar until creamy.

Add eggs and vanilla; beat well.

Add combined flour, baking soda and cinnamon; mix well.

Add oats and chocolate chips; mix well.

Drop by rounded tablespoons onto ungreased cookie sheets.

Bake 10 to 12 minutes or until golden brown. Cool 1 minute on cookie sheet; remove to wire rack. Cool completely.

Makes approximately 4 dozen cookies

ABOUT THE AUTHOR

Author photo by: Mikifoto – Mallika Malhotra

Judith Natelli McLaughlin has been writing for as long as she can remember. The first book she ever wrote is called *The Bunny and The Eggs*. She bound it with masking tape and her mother wrote *The End* in cursive. For Judith that was exactly how a real book was supposed to look.

She still loves to write and illustrate books but she no longer use masking tape to bind them. She publishes across genres. Books she has written include *Poems on Fruits & Odes to Veggies-Where Healthy Eating Starts With a Poem* and *This Moment*, "A beautiful piece of women's fiction." Candy Beauchamp – "Candy's Raves"

A native of New Jersey, Judith lives with her husband, Brian, her three daughters, Katie, Lindsay and Maggie and her faithful writing companion, a Westie named Duke.

www.judithnatellimclaughlin.com

CPSIA information can be obtained at www.ICGtesting.com
Printed in the USA
BVOW06s1927301015

424540BV00008B/147/P